ALBATROSS

by Martha Loader

Produced by Menagerie Theatre Company

Albatross was first performed on 28 April 2026 at Mercury Theatre, Colchester, followed by an East of England tour and a run at Omnibus Theatre, London.

An earlier version of *Albatross* was developed for performance in July 2024 at the Hotbed Festival, Cambridge Junction.

ALBATROSS

by Martha Loader

Cast

Eve	Agnes Lillis
Alice	Caroline Rippin
Martin	Patrick Morris

Creative and Production Team

Director	Patrick Morris
Designer	Chris Dobrowolski
Lighting Designer	Paul Bourne
Composer and Sound Designer	Michaela Polakova
Technical Stage Manager	Emma Chandler
Marketing Associate	Sarah Saxby

Production Credits

Dramaturgical Support	Steve Waters
Lighting Consultant	Ashley Day
Marketing Consultant	Karen Goddard
Print Design	Geoff Shirley
Film maker for trailer	Elena Morris-Gray
Student Placement	Dimitra Filippa

Menagerie Theatre Company

Artistic Directors	Paul Bourne and Patrick Morris
Board of Trustees	James Barlow, Kay Blayney and Rebecca Myers

Acknowledgements

We are immensely grateful to the following individuals and organisations who have contributed time, thought, resources, expertise and support to this production. You know what you did and we know we could not have done it without you:

Dr Amélie Kirchgaessner and Nopi Exizidou of British Antarctic Survey; Professor Steve Waters, Sarah Nacmanson and the team at UEA; Matt Burman and Jessica Weston-Snee of Cambridge Junction; Dr Joel Chalfen of Homerton College; Dr Andrew Burton; Professor Ian Willis; Professor John King; Dr Jonathan Croose of ARU; Catherine and Peter Rawlings; Helen Gould; Gerry Theobald.

We would like to thank the actors who were involved in the development of *Albatross* in 2024/25: Hayley Carmichael, Michael Lambourne, Hannah Ringham, Eric Colvin, Mike Bernadin.

Finally, thank you also to our wonderful Menagerie Supporters who donate money on an annual basis.

The following organisations provided funding for the production: Arts Council England, Unity Theatre Trust and the Sylvia Waddilove Foundation.

The production also received in-kind support from the British Antarctic Survey and the University of East Anglia.

Cast

Agnes Lillis | Eve

Agnes has worked in theatre for 40 years, starting at The Cockpit Theatre in Marylebone with Monstrous Regiment in *Points of Convergence*.

Neil Simon's comedy *Plaza Suite* followed at The English theatre of Hamburg, then a summer season with John Inman at The Jersey Opera House, after that she was understudy for the 3 young stars of *'Allo 'Allo!* at The London Palladium, which led to her being offered the role of Helga with the TV cast in Blackpool. Roles for The Seagull rep include Sybil in *Fawlty Towers* and Geraldine in *The Vicar of Dibley*. She especially enjoyed two tours for the acclaimed theatre company Eastern Angles *The Last Laugh* and *Another Three Sisters* directed by Ivan Cutting.

Other notable roles include Martha in *Who's Afraid of Virginia Woolf?* directed by Bernard Hill and Kate in *Dancing at Lughnasa*, acting alongside and directed by her long-time partner, the late Tony Scannell, for Eastbound theatre.

Patrick Morris | Martin

Co-founder and Co-Artistic Director of Menagerie.

He has directed *Albatross*, *The Great Austerity Debate*, *Four For Jericho*, *Correspondence*, *Let Newton Be!*, *The Retreating World* and *Between This Breath and You*. He runs Menagerie's Young Writers' Workshop and directs community/public art projects, most recently *The Trials of Democracy: Who Gives a XXXX?* He also runs The Ideas Stage, currently collaborating with Oxford and Sheffield Universities. Previous collaborations: *The Revival of Huntly Carter* with Oxford University; *The Good Death Project* and *The Great Austerity Debate* with Cambridge University, and *Human Rights! Bloody Human Rights!* with Queen Mary University of London.

As an actor, Menagerie credits include *bloominauschwitz, Bliss, Out of Your Knowledge, Re:Design, Frobisher's Gold, Hard Sell* and *The Cull*. Other acting credits include NIE, Foursight Theatre, The Public Theatre in New York, Magic Theatre in San Francisco.

Caroline Rippin | Alice

Caroline trained at Bretton Hall and is an actor, director and dramaturg.

Theatre credits include: *The Trials of Democracy* (Menagerie); *Phoenix, Dodo, Butterfly* (LJHope productions); *Splinter* (Brockley

Jack, Colchester Mercury); *The Handover* (Hotbed); *Bliss* (Finborough Theatre); *Phenomenon* (Hotbed); *The Great Austerity Debate* (Menagerie, National Tour); *What Country, Friends, is This?* (Hotbed Festival); *The Summer Before Everything* (Oxford Playhouse); *Pictures of You* (Soho Theatre); *A Workhouse Christmas* (Jumped Up Theatre); *Let Newton Be* (Menagerie); *Four for Jericho* (The Junction); *Stand By Your Van* (Pleasance Grand); *A Sudden Visitation of Calamity* (Hotbed); *Frobisher's Gold* (The Shaw); *Stormin' Jack Norman* (Theatre 503); *Michelle and The Landlady* (Pleasance); *Motherf**ker Island, In the White Highlands* (Drama Centre); *Blagger* (Teatro Piccolo); *White Nights* (The Spot, Covent Garden). Directed: *Doghead Boy and Sharkmouth go to Ikea, Blacklight* and *Oran's Message* (Menagerie); *Return Of The Vanishing Peasant* (Colchester Mercury); *Fallible* (Hotbed).

Creative and Production Team

Paul Bourne | Lighting Designer

Co-founder and Co-Artistic Director of Menagerie.

Previously Artistic Director at the Frankfurt Playhouse and Center Stage New York, Paul has directed and produced over sixty professional productions in ten different countries. Highlights include *Guignol* (Tennessee Williams) in New York, and the European premiere of *Oleanna* (David Mamet) in Frankfurt. For Menagerie he has directed a dozen productions for regional and national touring including *Frobisher's Gold* (Fraser Grace), *Hard Sell* (Craig Baxter), *The Cull* and *Out of Your Knowledge* (Steve Waters), *Egusi Soup* (Janice Okoh), *Swimming* (Jane Upton) and the international touring productions of *Bliss* (Fraser Grace) and *Hold On!* (Writer and Director; Most Municipal Theatre, Czech Republic).

Emma Chandler | Technical Stage Manager

Emma is a freelance Stage Manager and Theatre Technician from Lancashire.

She is excited to be returning to Cambridgeshire and the South East after training at the ADC Theatre during her degree and working with 62 Gladstone Street in Peterborough as the Stage Manager for the R&D of *The Table* by Aisha Zia last summer. Recent credits include Technical Operator for Darkfield's *Radio* and *Eulogy* at the Edinburgh Fringe, Assistant Stage Manager for *Snow White and the Seven Dwarves* at the Rotherham Civic Theatre, and Assistant Stage Manager for *Trial by Jury* at Garsington Studios.

Chris Dobrowolski | Designer

Chris studied Fine Art in Hull and when he first got there he built a boat from driftwood to try to escape. The boat failed but Chris ended up making a whole series of vehicles in a similar vein.

These included a sledge made from gold picture frames on an artist's residencey with the British Antarctic Survey. Over the years, Chris has retold and refined these stories as both artist and teacher. The result is a performance that translates the experience of creating and testing a theory. This in turn enables an audience to share and participate in a journey of discovery. Chris' latest show *Toy Stories* was created with Menagerie.

Martha Loader | Writer

Martha is an award-winning writer, actor and producer based in Ipswich. Her work has been performed across the UK and internationally.

She won the Judges Award at The Bruntwood Prize for Playwriting, 2022 for her play *Bindweed* and was nominated as a writer at The Stage Debut Awards, 2024. Her play *The Town* won the George Devine Award, 2025. Martha is also an alumnus of the 4Screenwriting and BBC Voices programmes. She is currently on attachment with the National Theatre and New Wolsey Theatre.

Patrick Morris | Director

See biography above.

Michaela Polakova | Composer and Sound Designer

Michaela Polakova is a Czech-born composer, producer, singer-songwriter, and pianist based in England, where she has lived for the past nineteen years.

She trained at the Prague Conservatoire, the University of East London, and King's College London. Her theatre work includes music and sound design for *Albatross* and *Bliss* (produced by Menagerie for the Hotbed Festival and Finborough Theatre) and *The Night Before the Funeral* (produced by Švanda Theatre in Prague). Michaela's film composition credits include the short film *Lurker*, created for the ARRI Trinity/ Directors UK One Shot Challenge. As a singer-songwriter, composer, and producer, she has credits on various albums released by Sony Music and Warner Music. In her music, Michaela blends influences from classical, electronic, and alternative pop genres, creating a distinctive and evocative sound.

Sarah Saxby | Marketing Associate

Sarah Saxby is a socially engaged writer, actor, and producer hailing from the Fens.

She graduated in 2022 from the University of Kent and in the same year founded Sticks Theatre, through whom she produced her first full length play, *Fourteen in '14*, as part of the 2024 Lambeth Fringe. She has been working with Menagerie Theatre Company since January 2024 and has worked with multiple organisations across the East of England including Metal Culture, Norfolk & Norwich Festival and Peterborough Presents. Sarah's work as a socially engaged artist draws heavily from her identity as someone from East Anglia and explores issues uniquely impacting those from the region.

Menagerie has been producing and developing award-winning theatre and live performance for over 25 years. Over that time, we have worked with hundreds of writers, performers, communities and organisations. Always open to new ideas and challenges, we have toured plays and worked with companies both nationally and internationally, from our home base at Cambridge Junction.

Menagerie promotes, develops and produces new plays through our Hotbed Festival, the Young Writers' Workshop and the Hidden Voices programme. Since 2001 we have supported hundreds of writers, particularly those based in the East of England. We build long-lasting relationships with playwrights, offering them a space for creative growth – from nationally-regarded writers such as Steve Waters, Fraser Grace and Naomi Wallace to early career artists like Janice Okoh, James McDermott and Martha Loader. Throughout this time our Artistic Directors Patrick Morris and Paul Bourne have maintained a clear mission: to breathe life into brave new work and provide opportunities for writers to reach audiences.

Connect with us:

Website www.menagerie.uk.com

Instagram @MenagerieTheatreCo

Facebook @MenagerieTheatreCompany

BlueSky @MenagerieTheatre.bsky.social

ALBATROSS

Martha Loader

'Is it he?' quoth one, 'Is this the man?
By him who died on cross,
With his cruel bow he laid full low
The harmless Albatross.

'The Rime of the Ancient Mariner'
Samuel Taylor Coleridge

Acknowledgements

Thanks to:

The Menagerie Theatre team and creatives.

Dr Natalie Robinson, Dr Morgan Seag, Professor Elizabeth Leane, Dr Rebecca Dell, Dr Amélie Kirchgaessner, Professor Elizabeth Morris OBE, Dr Leo Middleton, Dr Aoife O'Leary McNeice, Dr Oliver Marsh and Dr Rowan Whittle.

Professor Steve Waters, Imogen Greenberg, Dr Andrew Burton, Ben Musgrave, Hayley Carmichael, Michael Lambourne, Hannah Ringham and Eric Michael Colvin.

Mark Starling, Lily Williams and Diana Glazer.

M.L.

For all the mums.
Particularly my own.

Characters

EVE, *female, sixty-four*
ALICE, *female, thirty-nine*
MARTIN, *male, fifty-seven*

Notes

(,) indicates a beat when alone in a line. A beat is shorter than a pause. It can also denote a shift in thought or energy.

(/) indicates overlapping speech.

(…) indicates a trailing-off.

Dialogue in brackets indicates an aside.

No final punctuation indicates an interruption, either by another line of thought or another character.

This text went to press before the end of rehearsals and so may differ slightly from the play as performed.

Eve's kitchen. A 1980s house in a small town about seven miles north of Cambridge. A 'Live, Laugh, Love' sign hangs on the wall. Once neatly designed and immaculately maintained, there is something a bit 'off' about it. A lingering smell of damp. The floors look a bit weathered. There are watermarks up some of the cupboard doors. On a small table off to one side sits a large, stuffed albatross.

EVE *is clearing away the remnants of a candlelit dinner. An attempt at opulence in an otherwise rather sad environment. She takes off the tablecloth and folds it, extremely precisely. She looks at the albatross. It looks back at her.*

EVE. I thought they weren't real.

MARTIN (*off*). What?

EVE. Albatrosses. I thought they weren't real.

MARTIN (*off*). Hang on.

EVE. Or extinct maybe. Are they not extinct?

    The sound of a toilet flushing from off.

    MARTIN *enters, doing up his flies.*

MARTIN. What's extinct?

EVE. Alabtrosses.

    Or is it Albatross? Plural. Like sheep are sheep if there's one of them or lots of them.

MARTIN (*thinks*). Albatrosses. Yes I think, I think you were right the first time.

EVE. So they are real?

MARTIN. Well… yes.

EVE. Right. I just always thought, I dunno. Always thought they were made up. Like a phoenix or a dodo.

MARTIN. Dodos are real.

EVE. *Are they?*

MARTIN. Well not anymore. They're extinct.

EVE. But albatrosses aren't?

MARTIN. I don't think so.

EVE. Oh.

   '

Will we see them?

MARTIN. I don't know. I presume so. Penguins definitely, they said. But not, I'm not sure about albatrosses.

EVE. We can ask her tomorrow. When she's back. See what she reckons.

MARTIN. Yes.

EVE. I suppose we'll see all sorts.

MARTIN. Hopefully.

EVE. I'd like to see an elephant.

MARTIN. Oh. I don't think we'll

We might not

EVE. Not on this trip, no. No, of course. But just

One day.

In the wild, I mean. Not in the

I could just go to the zoo if I wanted to

MARTIN. Yes.

EVE. Loads of the buggers there.

I just think it must be different seeing them in the wild. In their natural habitat. Not in the freezing cold, next to a llama, with a Starbucks and a children's play area ten feet away.

   '

I just think that must be nice.

MARTIN. Yes.

EVE. But I'm looking forward to seeing penguins too.

MARTIN. Me too.

EVE. When I was much younger, in my dancing days, we did a whole show about penguins.

MARTIN. Did you?

EVE. I told you, didn't I? About me being a dancer.

MARTIN. You did, yes.

EVE. A whole show about them. Quite the unexpected hit it was too. Toured all around the North, we did. Hull, Bradford, Rochdale. Even made it to Blackpool which was quite a

Well, you'll know from *Strictly*, quite a big deal.

MARTIN. That's right.

EVE. All the men were dressed in suits, you know *penguin suits*, and us girls were in little black cocktail dresses with a white frilly panel down the front. All a bit of fun but, as I say, a real surprise box office smash as it turned out.

MARTIN. Sounds wonderful.

EVE. Well, yes. A lifetime ago now though. I used to travel all over the place then. The UK mostly, but sometimes abroad. This will be the furthest I've ever gone though. Will it for you?

MARTIN. Yes. Haven't been beyond Europe.

EVE. Oh the things we'll see.

,

I was thinking of packing a kettle maybe. Is that mad?

MARTIN. A kettle?

EVE. Yea. Maybe that's mad. I just, I go a bit loopy if I don't have a cup of tea in the morning. You know, as the first thing I do. So I just thought, maybe a travel kettle? We could keep it in the room. In the cabin.

MARTIN. We could, yes. But

EVE. But then I don't know what to do about milk. Do you think they'll have milk?

MARTIN. On the cruise?

EVE. Yes, of course. Silly question.

MARTIN. There'll be a whole dining area. *Areas*. You'll be able to get anything you like.

EVE. All through the day though? Because I do also like a cup of tea in the afternoon.

MARTIN. Yes, I think you'll be

EVE. I'll just take one. I'll take the kettle. Just to be on the safe side.

MARTIN. Okay.

Pause.

EVE. I think I'll wait to tell her. You know. About us going away. I think I'll wait a few days. After she's back.

MARTIN. Oh?

EVE. She can be a bit

And she sounded funny. You know. On the phone. She's always a bit funny when she first gets back.

MARTIN. Okay, but

EVE. Not too long. Just a day or so. Just to let her settle back in.

MARTIN. Because we go next Friday.

EVE. I know. I know, but I just

I just think I'll, that she'll

That it'll just be better this way.

MARTIN. Okay, well. Whatever you think is best.

EVE *goes to* MARTIN *and puts her arms around him.*

EVE. What are you most looking forward to? On the trip.

MARTIN. Spending time with you.

EVE. Give over.

MARTIN. I am! I'm looking forward to getting to know you better. Just the two of us.

EVE. That's nice.

Do you think I'll like the food? I don't know what kind of food it'll be down there.

MARTIN. All sorts I imagine. Probably a buffet.

EVE. Really? Oh, I just go mad for a buffet.

MARTIN. They've got food from every nationality apparently.

EVE. Oh yeah?

MARTIN. Italian, Chinese, Japanese

She kisses him.

EVE. Oh, Martin.

MARTIN. Mediterranean.

EVE. You're making me giddy.

MARTIN. Salad bars, pizza by the slice. An omelette station.

She kisses him again.

EVE. Oh, Martin! I can't wait.

MARTIN. Me neither.

She goes to kiss him again.

A cry from upstairs.

EVE. Oh god.

(*Grimaces.*) Sorry. I'd better see what that's about.

MARTIN. Do you have to?

EVE. She'll only come down.

MARTIN *kisses her this time.*

MARTIN. Are you sure?

EVE *hesitates.*

Another cry from upstairs.

EVE. I'll be back in two ticks. Don't go anywhere.

She exits.

A moment of stillness as MARTIN *is left alone.*

Then he looks towards the albatross. It looks at him.

He goes to it, reaches out a hand to touch it.

The lights flicker.

*

A little while later. The kitchen is now dark. The lights are off. Cutting through the black, the sound of two people rutting. Perhaps we're not quite sure what we're hearing at first but then it becomes abundantly clear.

After a moment, the main light is switched on to reveal EVE *and* MARTIN, *illuminated in the suddenly piercing light, in an extremely compromising position – up against the cabinets maybe, or over the dining table. And in the doorway, hand still on the light switch is* ALICE, *a large rucksack on her back, her mouth open.*

There is silence for a moment as EVE *and* MARTIN *look towards* ALICE, *and* ALICE *looks at them.*

ALICE (*horrified*). Mum!

EVE (*delighted*). Alice! You're back.

ALICE. Oh my god. Oh my shitting, fucking / god

EVE. I wasn't expecting you so soon.

    EVE *and* MARTIN *separate themselves.*

ALICE. I can see that.

    ,

    What's

    Who's *he?*

    She points at MARTIN.

EVE. / Martin.

MARTIN. / I'm Martin.

ALICE. *Who?*

EVE. *Martin.* I told you about Martin.

ALICE. No you bloody

EVE. Well I thought I did.

    Pause.

    Then MARTIN *goes towards* ALICE, *hand outstretched.*

MARTIN. You must be Alice, I've heard so much about

ALICE (*recoiling*). Oh my god, please don't touch me / after

MARTIN. Oh. Oh right, no of of

ALICE. Jesus.

    He backs off again. Almost reversing.

MARTIN. Sorry.

    ,

    We were just

    We weren't

    Just now. We weren't

ALICE. Are you kidding?

EVE. Don't, Martin. She's not an idiot.

MARTIN. No.

ALICE. No, I know *exactly* what you

EVE. Besides. We're all adults here, aren't we? All heard of sex before, / haven't we?

ALICE. / Oh my god.

EVE. Well haven't we?

Nothing to be ashamed of, is there?

ALICE. Well not on my part.

Pause.

EVE. How was your journey? My darling. I'd have picked you up from the airport if I'd known.

Want a tea? Why don't we all have tea?

She looks at MARTIN *who tries to smile supportively.*

ALICE *ignores her.*

ALICE. So he's what, your *boyfriend*, is he?

EVE. / No.

MARTIN. / That's right.

Oh.

EVE. Well, we haven't put a label on it yet.

MARTIN. Right.

ALICE. Just keeping it casual, are you?

,

How long have you been

EVE. Not long.

MARTIN. A few months.

ALICE. A few months?

(*To* EVE.) You have been busy. I can't have been five minutes out the door before you

EVE. Don't, Alice.

ALICE. What?

EVE. Acting like a teenager. You're a grown woman

ALICE. I'm

EVE. As am I.

,

I fancy a hot chocolate. Anyone else for a hot choccy?

ALICE. And where did you meet?

EVE (*exasperated*). Oh, Alice.

MARTIN. Online.

ALICE. On –

I didn't think you even knew about online dating.

EVE. Of course I do. I'm not a complete neanderthal. Tish from Legs, Bums and Tums has been doing it for years.

ALICE. Yes but her husband ran off with the window cleaner! This is different.

EVE. Of course it's not.

(*Hisses.*) And I'm not discussing this in front of Martin.

ALICE. Well Martin might want to leave then, mightn't he?

A small standoff.

MARTIN. Er yes. I think I'll

Maybe go upstairs for a while?

EVE. Why don't you run down to the all night Tescos? Get us a bottle of something.

,

(*Prompting.*) To celebrate.

MARTIN. Oh yes, our

EVE. *Alice's return.*

She gives him a look.

MARTIN. Yes, of course.

He nods and starts backing out.

EVE. Martin?

He reappears in the doorway.

MARTIN. Yes?

EVE. Keys.

She takes them from the sideboard and gives them to him.

(*Quietly.*) Just not tonight.

He nods and leaves.

ALICE *narrows her eyes at* EVE *suspiciously.*

ALICE. What was that about?

EVE. Oh nothing.

Martin doesn't drink so I was just giving him a suggestion.

ALICE. Is he an alcoholic?

EVE. No.

ALICE. You've asked an alcoholic to go and buy alcohol?

EVE. No!

You're being very rude.

ALICE. Me?

EVE. I'm sure it was a

Well a bit of a surprise. Not the way I planned on you two meeting certainly but

ALICE. What about Dad?

EVE. That's not

This has nothing to do with / Derek.

ALICE. You've told him, have you? That you're recently widowed?

EVE. Not recently, Alice. It's been over a year.

ALICE. Just.

EVE. Martin has been extremely supportive these last few months. He's been nice company for me. I do still have needs you know.

ALICE. Oh god, gross.

EVE. And it's not like I've had you to talk to. It can get quite lonely. With you away. And what with your dad.

And Alba.

A moment. A sharp electrical current through ALICE.

So.

,

Let's just drop it. Shall we?

Pause.

ALICE. Fine.

EVE *raises an eyebrow.*

Yes, okay. Fine.

EVE. Ohh it is lovely to have you home. Not expecting you back for at least another

ALICE. I know.

EVE. I'd have made up your bed if I'd known.

ALICE. I know. I should have called.

EVE. Doesn't

ALICE. Sorry.

EVE. Doesn't matter at all. It's a treat to have you back so soon.

ALICE *looks around her, finally taking in the state of the kitchen.*

ALICE. Oh my

What's happened?

EVE. What?

ALICE. Here. The kitchen is

What happened?

EVE. Oh. Flooded. A few weeks back.

ALICE. Oh my god.

EVE. I've cleaned it up best I could. But it's

ALICE. Shit, it's

Really bad. The cupboards are

EVE. Yes.

ALICE. What about the rest of the street?

EVE. Got everyone. Sue and Gary, Denise and Sarah. Marcus
has had to move out. We had one of those industrial de- de-

ALICE. Dehumidifiers?

EVE. That's right. But it's still

Well you can smell it.

ALICE. Yeah, god.

EVE. I light a candle most evenings. A smelly. But

I can't quite bear to look at it to be honest.

ALICE. I'm sure.

,

Sorry.

I didn't realise.

EVE. That's okay. We carry on.

She goes to ALICE *and holds her face in her hands.*

It's so good to have you back. My darling. Did you get
a taxi?

ALICE. Yes.

EVE. From the station?

ALICE. Yes.

EVE. Must have cost a bit, I'd have picked you up from the airport if I'd known.

ALICE. It's fine.

EVE. Having to drag your stuff across London. Then all the way back here. Come into Heathrow, did you?

ALICE. Er, yeah. Yup.

EVE. Stansted would have been easier.

ALICE. Well, planes from Chile don't tend to come into Stansted.

EVE. No.

,

No, I suppose not.

Want to bring your stuff in properly? We'll trip over that in the morning.

ALICE. I will, I was just

EVE. Leaving it in the doorway like that isn't

ALICE. I know.

EVE. It's a trip hazard.

ALICE. Well I was a bit distracted before.

EVE *holds up her hands.*

EVE. Touché.

ALICE*'s phone pings.*

She looks at it quickly.

Fancy that cuppa?

ALICE. What?

EVE. Cuppa. I'll stick on the kettle.

ALICE. Oh.

She puts her phone away.

Maybe something stronger.

EVE. Oh yeah?

ALICE. Any of Dad's whiskey left?

She goes to one of the cupboards and rummages around.

EVE. Oh I don't know actually. Haven't been drinking much lately.

ALICE. No?

EVE. Well, as Martin doesn't

ALICE. (Because he's an alcoholic.)

EVE. He's not an alcoholic. He's a spiritualist.

ALICE. A what?

EVE. You know. Believes in the Universe and such.

ALICE. Well the Universe does exist I suppose, so

EVE. You know what I mean, Alice. And, well. He says alcohol gets in the way of his connectivity.

ALICE. His connectivity?

EVE. Yes. So I

You know, don't really feel the need for it either. Can feel a bit odd, can't it? Drinking on your own.

ALICE. Mm.

EVE. You may scoff, but it's not all

Some of it's quite

You know.

He's got me into all sorts. He's into this

Clean living. Is that what it's called? Fresh veg and oily fish. Raw stuff. I thought it was all a bit, you know, a bit woo-woo at first but I

Now I'm quite enjoying it.

ALICE. Right.

EVE. I've lost five pounds.

ALICE. Wow.

EVE. He doesn't

I know he doesn't look the type. But he's been through some things, Martin and he says, he says reevaluating his life, changing his diet, his outlook has

Well, has potentially saved his life. And you can't argue with that, can you?

ALICE. I'm sure I could give it a go.

ALICE *tries a final cupboard and finds what she's looking for.*

Aha!

She pulls out a bottle of whiskey.

Looks at the label and gives a low whistle.

Jesus this stuff is practically 100% ethanol.

Will you?

EVE. No. No, I shouldn't.

EVE *watches as* ALICE *pours herself a large measure and drinks.*

I'll get you a glass of water to go with it.

ALICE. I don't

EVE. I'll just get you one.

She pulls another glass out of the cupboard and a large bottle of water from under the sink.

ALICE. Bottled?

EVE. Not safe to drink from the taps since the

ALICE. Ah.

> EVE *places the water down in front of* ALICE.
>
> *She watches until* ALICE *takes a drink.*

EVE. Best to drink lots of water after a long flight too. Dehydrates you all that.

ALICE. Yeah. Yeah, that's

EVE. And certainly if you drink in the middle of the night. Ages you prematurely. Dehydration is the silent killer of collagen. I drink eight glasses a day now. Religiously. I feel wonderful for it.

ALICE. Well

,

Great.

> EVE *picks up the whiskey bottle and looks at it.*

EVE. Tell you one thing, he wasn't a snob, your father.

ALICE. No.

EVE. Never minded the cheap stuff, Derek. The own brand.

ALICE. Actively despised the expensive stuff. Ruined his Dr Pepper, remember?

EVE. That's right! a pint of whiskey and Dr Pepper on a Friday night.

ALICE. Surprised he lived as long as he did.

EVE. Yes, well.

> *Silence.*

ALICE. Mum…

EVE. So what do you think of him?

ALICE. Who?

EVE. Martin!

ALICE. Oh, yeah. He seems

EVE. He's actually a bit younger than me.

ALICE. *Is he?*

EVE. Yes.

   He's only fifty-seven.

ALICE. Gosh.

EVE. That's in your age bracket too, these days.

ALICE. No it's bloody not.

EVE. Well you're hardly a spring chicken.

ALICE. Cheers.

   EVE *laughs and kisses* ALICE *on the head.*

EVE. Oh your hair's got long. Got awfully long.

ALICE. Well, not many hairdressers down there.

EVE. And scraggly. All your ends are split. Won't catch a man
   looking like that.

ALICE. Right. Not the main reason I'm there, but sure.

   She smiles.

   They used to use that as an excuse actually. No hairdressers
   in Antarctica. That was one of the reasons they didn't let
   women go in the early days. No shops or hairdressers for the
   poor little ladies.

EVE. It would put me off.

ALICE. God's sake.

EVE. Don't get me wrong, I'm sure it's beautiful.

   But months of it. What do you *do*?

ALICE. We work.

EVE. Sure but

It must get, you know, after a while.

ALICE. We read a lot. Watch a bit of telly. People knit.

EVE. Christ.

ALICE. You're mostly too exhausted to do anything.
Particularly this time. This time it was actually really

EVE. I can imagine. I'm exhausted just thinking about it.

And all those people, for so long. I don't know how you
stand it.

ALICE. How do you mean?

EVE. Oh I'd go mad. Not having my own space. With the same
people day in, day out. I'd throttle someone. Throw them
into a crevasse. People go all loopy out there, don't they?
Didn't one of Captain Scott's lot take all his clothes off?
Delirious from the weather. Hypothermia makes you think
you're hot when you're actually freezing to death.

ALICE. Yeah, I think so. Funny you remember that.

EVE. Oh you used to love those stories about Scott when
you were little, didn't you? You and your dad. I found
some of your old storybooks about him in the attic while
I was putting Derek's stuff up there. You were obsessed.
Remember? Height of summer, you used to go around in
your big coat, two bits of cardboard strapped to your shoes,
pulling that old milk crate behind you like a sledge. Lord
knows what the neighbours thought.

She laughs.

I suppose it never left you.

ALICE *looks warmly at* EVE.

A moment of recognition between them.

ALICE. No. No, I suppose not.

EVE *shudders violently.*

EVE. Ooh I got a

Right through me. Went all cold suddenly. Creeps up on you, doesn't it?

Warmest, wettest February on record here they reckon. Not that you'd know it. I wear a bobble hat to bed now. Thermal long johns, hot water bottle and a bobble hat.

ALICE. Sounds sensible.

EVE. Sounds bloody depressing, is what it does. It's what they did in the 1920s. Not the 2020s.

ALICE. Yea, well…

EVE. Bloody depressing.

Don't know how you stand it out there for so long.

ALICE. Well. No, but

It's different.

EVE. Less rain.

ALICE. Yeah

EVE. And you're prepared for the cold out there, I suppose.

ALICE. Yeah, but

Well it's a different kind of cold. It's drier. Less humid.

(*Laughs.*) First time I went, I was wrapped up to the hilt. Just my eyes showing through my snowsuit.

EVE. They got you to put on that massive outfit on the plane.

ALICE. That's right. And when we stepped out onto the runway, we were all boiling.

EVE. And they were all laughing at you. The people who'd spent the winter there.

ALICE. Ha, yeah.

EVE. They were just in their fleeces.

ALICE. Barely a coat between them.

They laugh.

EVE. I always tell people that story.

ALICE. Do you?

She looks at EVE, *slightly surprised.*

That's nice.

,

I mean obviously it's bloody freezing sometimes. It felt colder doing fieldwork this time round.

EVE. Even though it's supposedly getting hotter down there?

ALICE. It is. It is getting warmer. But a couple of degrees difference to the air temperature doesn't mean much when you're getting hit in the face by a blizzard.

EVE. Oh god. You're making it sound awful!

ALICE. No, it's

If you could see it, Mum. It's a whole other world down there.

,

We took a boat out this time. When we first arrived. Sailed around all these icebergs. Whales everywhere you look. Penguins leaping out of the water like dolphins.

,

I can't really explain it, Mum. It's

She stops.

Looks a bit glassy-eyed.

EVE. I suppose you just have to go to understand?

ALICE. Maybe. Yeah.

ALICE has another large swig of her drink.

Something catches her eye, and she suddenly notices the albatross.

The lights flicker.

Oh my

What the bloody hell is that?

EVE. Oh yes. Martin bought it.

ALICE. He

What? Is it a, a

ALICE *stares at it.*

EVE. An albatross. Yes! They're real apparently.

ALICE. Of course they're real. What's it doing in my house?

EVE. *Our* house. It was a gift.

ALICE. A gift? Is that a joke?

EVE. Of course not. It's a nice thing for him to do.

ALICE. Nice? It's *horrible.* Why would I want a reminder of their imminent extinction in my kitchen?

EVE. *Our* kitchen. And that's not, that's obviously not what it is. You should like it. It's science.

ALICE. It's weird. It's a weird thing to give as a present. Most new step-parents bring toys or sweets, don't they? Not *taxidermy.*

EVE. Oh shush. Anyway, it's not *for* you. It's for me.

ALICE. Why would you want it?

EVE. And for Alba.

Electricity.

Alba the albatross. That's what I call her, isn't it, so… He thought we'd like it. We'd *all* like it.

ALICE. Huh.

EVE. Just be nice about it when he gets back. Okay?

,

Okay?

ALICE. Fine. Yes, okay.

Pause.

EVE. You look tired, my love.

ALICE. Thanks.

EVE. You hungover?

ALICE. Hungover?

EVE. Not hungover. What do I mean?

ALICE. Jetlagged?

EVE. That's it. Feels the same though, doesn't it?

ALICE. When have you ever been jetlagged? You've barely been beyond Malaga.

EVE. I went to the States. When I was younger.

ALICE. Right, yeah but

EVE. I danced / out there.

ALICE. / Danced out there, yes. I remember. But

EVE. Well I did. Long before your time of course.

Lot you don't know about me. There was life before kids you know.

ALICE. I remember.

EVE. Yes, well, you had longer. Longer on your own, doing your own thing, than I did.

ALICE. I know.

EVE. Twenty-four when I got pregnant with you.

ALICE. I know.

EVE. Twenty-five when I had you. No age.

ALICE. It's young. By today's standards / particularly

EVE. / By any standards. I'm not that old.

ALICE. Well I'm nearly forty…

EVE. Barely got started with life at twenty-four. Whereas you

Nearly thirty-five by the time you had Alba.

A beat. Another electric shock.

ALICE. ,

Yeah.

EVE. Women having them in their forties now. The life I could have lived if I'd waited.

I'd probably be dead by now.

ALICE. Eh?

EVE. If I'd waited. Another twenty years, I could be dead.

ALICE. Well it's more that I'd be twenty years younger than / you'd be

EVE. / Dead and buried. Or at least in a home.

ALICE (*laughs*). Christ! Okay, Mum.

Silence.

ALICE *looks at the albatross. It looks at her.*

It's not jetlag. Not just that anyway. I feel kind of wired. Haven't really slept in days. Weeks maybe.

EVE. Lot on the mind?

ALICE. Something like that.

EVE. Oh I'm the same. It's this weather. Months of it, we've had. Makes it impossible to sleep, when the rain's lashing down on the Velux. Makes you morbid all that.

ALICE. Yeah?

EVE. Though as Martin says, only a bit of weather.

ALICE. Well sort of, but

ALICE *looks at the ruined kitchen.*

More than just a bit of weather to do this.

EVE (*sadly*). Yes.

She points at a corner of the room.

I had to paint over Alba's height chart. Where she'd measured all her teddies.

She wells up a bit.

Looks at ALICE, who does not look at her.

Now might be the time to offer me a hug?

ALICE. Oh.

Oh, do you

Would you

EVE. Yes.

ALICE gets up and hugs her awkwardly.

EVE laughs.

ALICE. What?

EVE. Nothing, no.

ALICE. What?

EVE. You're so tense.

ALICE. I'm not.

EVE. Like hugging a tennis racket.

ALICE moves away from her.

Are you hungry? You *feel* hungry. When was the last time you ate?

ALICE. No, I'm

EVE. Skin and bones. I could make you some rice pudding? Alba loves rice pudding.

Another beat.

ALICE. Does she?

EVE. Just like you when you were little.

ALICE. That's nice.

EVE. Shall I put some on?

ALICE. Okay.

Yeah.

Thanks.

EVE goes to one of the cupboards and pulls out a tin of rice pudding.

She places a saucepan on the stove and empties the can into it.

She stirs as it warms.

EVE. You haven't asked.

ALICE. What?

EVE. About her. Since you got in.

,

Alba.

ALICE. Asked what?

EVE. About her. Not once.

ALICE. I spoke to her the other day. Before I knew I was coming back. Tried again this morning, but I guess she was

EVE. At school, yes.

ALICE. Right, so

,

How is she?

EVE. Fine, yes.

ALICE. Oh Mum!

EVE. What?

ALICE. You make this grand statement that I haven't asked after my daughter and then when I do ask, you just say 'fine'.

EVE. Well she is.

ALICE. Fine.

EVE. And hardly a *grand statement*, I just would have thought you'd want to know

ALICE. I do.

EVE. as soon as you came home

ALICE. I did

EVE. burning to rush upstairs and see her.

ALICE. She's asleep.

EVE. Hmph.

ALICE. Isn't she? She should be.

EVE. Yes of course she is. Of course she is, because I put her to bed at seven and I read her a bedtime story, *Bye Bye Baby*, and then she went to

ALICE. *Bye Bye Baby*?

EVE. Yes. She loves it. I love it. Used to make me cry.

ALICE. You read her a story

EVE. (Still does.)

ALICE. that begins, 'There was once a baby who had no mummy'?

EVE. Yes.

Well, no, I see what you're getting at but

ALICE. Oh, Mum for god's sake!

EVE. No, it wasn't meant to be

She loves it. It's a nice story. With a nice ending.

ALICE. It's about an abandoned child who has to look after themselves.

EVE. Until the end. Until the little adventure it goes on to find a / mummy

ALICE. / Christ!

EVE. Oh, don't.

ALICE. Not.

EVE. You are, you're twisting it into something / more

ALICE. / Something more? You're feeding her abandonment narratives!

EVE. *Abandonment narratives.* Not doing anything of the sort. It's a cartoon baby who makes friends with a cat and a clockwork hen, it's hardly

ALICE. She's going to hate me when she's older.

EVE. Oh stop.

ALICE. She will! You're giving her a complex.

EVE. Well you're the one that's been away for four months, it's hardly

Silence.

ALICE *looks at her lap.*

ALICE. Three.

Silence.

EVE *stirs the rice pudding.*

I had to come back early because we need more funding.

EVE. Oh?

ALICE. Yeah. It's quite serious actually.

EVE. Oh?

ALICE. An ice shelf near our research station looks like it might collapse. If it does, the station could be at risk so we've got to get more money to monitor it over winter.

EVE. Oh?

She's half listening while she stirs the pot.

ALICE. It's actually, well it's actually

It's something we've been modelling for a while. There's all this meltwater now, because it's so much warmer down there so it's

Well it's been putting quite a lot of pressure on the ice shelves, causing them to bend, buckle under the

But now they're starting to fracture, around the meltwater, and that will probably cause them to collapse. It's awful obviously, potentially catastrophic, but actually well, in some ways, quite exciting to see that our models are

She looks up, realises EVE *isn't listening.*

Mum?

EVE. Yes?

ALICE. ?

EVE. Yes, yes, sorry I'm listening. Ice shelves and stations and and penguins.

ALICE. I didn't say anything about penguins.

EVE. Right, no. Sorry, I think I'm crashing slightly. It's getting late.

ALICE. Yeah, yeah I know.

So, yeah, so what I'm saying is

If we get the funding, I might have to go back.

Back out there.

EVE *stops stirring the pot and looks around.*

EVE. To Antarctica?

ALICE. Yes.

EVE. When?

ALICE. Um

I'm not sure.

EVE. For how long?

ALICE. For

For a little while.

Maybe.

EVE. Well that's ridiculous. You have a daughter.

ALICE. I know.

EVE. You can't leave your daughter for another however long. You've been gone four months already.

ALICE. Three.

The rice starts to bubble up.

Mum.

EVE. Three.

ALICE. Mum, the rice is

EVE. Well you just tell them no.

ALICE. It's not that easy. It's my team. I'm responsible.

EVE. Surely you've got other people beneath you that can

ALICE. It's my job. It's what I've been working on for literally

EVE. Yes, but not to live out there permanently. That's not

ALICE. It's really important. If the shelf collapses, it's not just the base that's at risk. We actually don't know what might happen. It's an area the size of Greater London that could go. Imagine that being dumped into the ocean suddenly.

EVE. Yes, yes, we know all about that, Alice. Sea levels rising and no light at the end of the tunnel.

We're all very aware of just how important your work / is

ALICE. / Our house literally just flooded. You shouldn't be so dismissive.

EVE. We're nowhere near the sea here, Alice! It floods around here all the time. It's just

ALICE. Oh Mum, come on.

EVE. Not everything is (don't patronise me) is connected to you and your work.

ALICE. I'm not!

Mum, that rice is

EVE. Oh god.

EVE *stirs the rice pudding quickly.*

She takes it off the heat.

ALICE. And it *is*. Connected. Higher temperatures, more evaporation

EVE. Yeah, yeah.

ALICE. more rainfall, more flooding.

EVE. I *know*.

,

But actually.

Well there is some thinking that more rainfall could make some desert landscapes habitable suddenly. New places for people to live maybe. The Sahara Desert might become like… Portugal.

ALICE. Sorry?

EVE. Just an example.

ALICE. We can't predict where that rainfall will increase. Some of these places will probably get *hotter*, not suddenly turn into the Algarve.

EVE. I said, just an example.

ALICE *looks at her closely.*

ALICE. What have you been reading?

EVE. What? Oh no, nothing.

ALICE. Mum.

EVE. Nothing.

,

I listened to a podcast.

ALICE. Of course you did.

EVE. It was very interesting. Looking at the positives for once, not just the

You've got to keep an open mind.

ALICE. Not about this you don't.

EVE. Oh you're so

ALICE. Our. House. Flooded.

EVE. I *know*.

ALICE. What more proof do you

EVE. I *know*, Alice. It was *my* house. Not yours. Mine. Me that had to clear up the shit and mud and and

Water up to my ankles at one point. Filthy, stinking sewage that I was having to clear out with a broom, while you're off flying around the world, causing more damage in Antarctica with your big boats and your aeroplanes and your generators. More damage than you're solving.

Silence.

ALICE. Is that what you think?

EVE. I don't know.

ALICE. Where's this coming from?

EVE. Nowhere. It's nothing.

ALICE. Because you know you have to be careful with

EVE. I know.

ALICE. Lots of podcasts aren't

They're not based on, on anything real. Anyone can have / an opinion on

EVE. I know, Alice.

Just drop it, will you?

Silence.

ALICE. You said it was my house too earlier.

EVE. It is.

ALICE. I am sorry about what happened. About not being here to

I love this place as much as you do.

EVE. I know.

,

I know you do, love.

,

But with all of that happening with your dad gone and a five-year-old running round causing havoc…

,

Would have finished me off this flood I think. Were it not for Martin.

Silence.

EVE *switches the hob off.*

Grub's up.

EVE *gets some bowls from the drying rack.*

They are children's bowls – a Peter Rabbit design running around the edge.

She spoons rice pudding into each.

She puts them on the table.

Brings jam and cutlery too.

ALICE *takes in the bowl as it's handed to her.*

She turns it in her hands as she reads the little story on the inside lip.

ALICE. 'Then old Mrs. Rabbit took a basket and her umbrella, and went through the wood to the baker's. She bought a loaf of brown bread.'

,

These were mine. When I was little.

EVE. Yes.

ALICE. Does Alba

EVE. Yes. She loves them too. Wants to go as Peter Rabbit to World Book Day this year.

ALICE. That's nice.

EVE. Those ears have been a real bastard to make though.

She laughs.

ALICE *is silent.*

She spoons jam into the bowl and mixes it, but doesn't eat.

EVE *sits down and tucks in.*

Shouldn't really. Just had dinner. But it's

Well it's called pudding, isn't it? So

,

Just about all your dad could manage by the end, wasn't it? Rice pudding. Rice pudding with jam. With cinnamon. Even with sausages that time, remember?

She shudders.

You'd think I'd be sick of it by now. Swore I'd never touch it again after

After he

But the first night you left. This last time. That night Alba asked for it specially. And I thought, *Can't really say no, can I?* Not when it's hard finding food she actually likes. So when she asked I had to say yes. And I thought, I thought, *Sod it. I'll have it too.*

And it was

Well to be honest it sort of released something in me. Eating that rice pudding that night. For the first time I thought, *I can move on now.* Sounds strange, doesn't it? But it was like, and don't laugh, but it was like, *Well if I can eat rice pudding again without him and the world doesn't end... What else can I do without him?*

You know?

,

ALICE. Oh, Mum. You were a great wife to him.

EVE. Mm.

ALICE. You *were*. You cared for him for so long. And so brilliantly.

EVE. How would you know? You weren't here.

ALICE. I

I *was*. I was here for / months while

EVE. / Not when he died.

ALICE. Because I was, was working. It was the precursor to this trip, I couldn't

EVE. You could, Alice. You could have chosen to stay. With your dad, with Alba.

Electricity.

With me.

ALICE. He he told me to go.

EVE. Of course he did. Because it's always been that way. Alice and Derek's little club of two. I wasn't allowed a look in.

ALICE. That's not

EVE. Antarctica was his dream before it was yours. But neither of you were the ones looking after a sick husband all those years. Caring for a small child while he was dying in the next room. I barely slept that final month. I got shingles I was so run down. So don't, *He told me to go*, because that wasn't

That actually wasn't his choice to make, Alice.

Silence.

ALICE. I didn't realise.

EVE. No.

ALICE. Didn't know it had got that bad. You should have told me.

EVE. How?

ALICE. On the

Could have told me on the phone. I know I couldn't be there, but I could have shared some of that, that pain with you.

EVE. Oh Alice.

EVE *reaches out and touches* ALICE*'s cheek.*

You'll never truly understand that.

ALICE *moves her head away sharply.*

ALICE. Don't. Treating me like a child. I could have been there for you. If you'd let me.

EVE. You wouldn't know how. Love isn't just a biological reaction, Alice. A few chemicals whizzing around. It's got to cost something. You can't just say the words, you've got to really mean them.

ALICE. How can you

He was my dad too. I miss him just as much as

EVE. I know.

ALICE. You're making me out to be some kind of… robot.

I have a child, for god's sake.

EVE. And who raises her?

ALICE. That's

EVE. In the five years she's been alive, you've been away for nearly eight months. That's thirteen per cent of her life.

ALICE. I work! This is my

And wow, you've worked that to the decimal place, haven't you?

You know what I do might actually help buy Alba a future? All kids a future.

EVE. And what about the present? You're happy to forget about that, are you?

ALICE. Wh –

EVE. People have other things on their minds, Alice. Bills to pay, food to buy, *children to raise*. Your work isn't top of everyone's priority list. Sorry to break it to you.

ALICE. Are you

Is this

Are you winding me up?

EVE. No. I'm just saying, it's a difficult time for a lot of people at the moment. Your Arctic adventures

ALICE. Antarctic.

EVE. Your *Antarctic* adventures aren't on everyone's radar. And, well, it takes a certain degree of privilege to worry about these things.

ALICE. *Privilege?* Are you kidding? Where are you suddenly getting all this, all this… *bullshit* from?

EVE. Don't patronise me, Alice. I will not be patronised.

EVE *stands.*

ALICE. I'm not. You just, you don't seem to understand how serious this is. What it means.

EVE *walks towards the door leading upstairs.*

Mum.

What are you

Where are you going?

EVE. Upstairs.

ALICE. But

EVE. I need another layer.

And someone should probably check on your daughter.

EVE *exits.*

ALICE *sits in disbelief for a moment.*

She looks at the albatross. The albatross looks at her.

The lights flicker.

It begins to snow in the kitchen.

She stands, closes her eyes. The snow falls around her.

Then her phone buzzes.

The snow stops abruptly.

She hesitates, then answers.

ALICE. Yes.

She looks at the albatross. The albatross looks at her.

Yes, I'm there now.

,

I told you, I'm sorting it.

She closes her eyes, phone still to her ear.

I'm sorting it.

*

A little while later. ALICE *is slumped in an armchair, asleep.* MARTIN *appears in the doorway to the hall holding a plastic bag. He watches her sleep for a moment. Then* ALICE *wakes up. As if realising she's being watched.*

ALICE. Oh my god.

MARTIN. Sorry.

ALICE. Martin. Jesus, I thought

MARTIN. Sorry. Sorry, I didn't mean to

ALICE. It's fine. I'm just a bit

I just get a bit

Jumpy.

MARTIN. Of course.

ALICE. Takes me a bit of time to

You know, to adjust.

MARTIN. Of course.

Sorry, I didn't realise you were asleep.

ALICE. I wasn't. Not really. I don't really sleep much. At the moment.

MARTIN. I'm sure.

,

Sorry, I just wasn't sure how much time Eve wanted me to be out for

ALICE. It's fine.

MARTIN. And then it turned out that the all night Tescos actually isn't an all night Tescos.

ALICE. Oh, right.

MARTIN. So then I went to the Asda in the hope that that was, well, *all night.* Which it also isn't. But there was an off license next door where I managed to get some, er

He pulls out a bottle. Looks at the label.

Liebfraumilch.

,

So

He hands it to her.

I'm afraid I don't really drink very much these days.

ALICE. So I understand.

Well, er

Thanks, Martin.

Pause.

MARTIN. I fear we might have got off on the wrong foot before.

ALICE. Uh huh.

MARTIN. You see, we have a very deep connection, Eve and I.

ALICE. Yes. I witnessed that earlier.

MARTIN. I

Yes, and I feel I should

Should *explain* what

ALICE. Oh god, please don't. I'm a little too old for *The Talk*.

MARTIN. I just want you to know that, although it's early days, I am very serious about her.

ALICE. Is that why you bought her an albatross?

MARTIN. I

,

Well I

It was meant for all of you really. As a

ALICE. What?

MARTIN. As a gift.

ALICE. Right.

  Funny kind of gift.

  Silence.

MARTIN. Eve tells me you're a glaciologist.

ALICE. Yup.

MARTIN. Well, I think that's rather amazing.

ALICE. Do you?

MARTIN. Yes! I mean, I don't really know, don't understand everything that you

  What it is exactly that you do. But your research into ice shelf stability and fracture processes I thought was

ALICE. Did *Mum* tell you that?

MARTIN. Well, I'll admit, I looked that bit up.

ALICE. Huh.

MARTIN. But I was, I was following your tweets with great interest.

ALICE (*taken aback*). Were you?

MARTIN. Oh yes. I got Twitter just so I could

  X now, isn't it?

ALICE. Sure.

MARTIN. Well, I got that just so that I could follow your progress. I mean obviously just the layman's stuff.

ALICE. Right.

MARTIN. But the work you're doing on the meltwater causing the ice to fracture is is fascinating.

ALICE. God.

  ,

  Right.

MARTIN. I might have got that wrong.

ALICE. No, it's

That's it. Basically.

,

I mean I don't know how much you

MARTIN. No please.

ALICE. Well we've modelled it for years. But this is the closest we've come to actually observing it happen.

MARTIN. Fantastic.

ALICE. It's probably what caused the Larsen B Ice Shelf to collapse about twenty years ago? So it's, you know, it's quite exciting.

Quite devastating too of course, but

She frowns at him. Unsure.

Anyway. I won't bore you with it all.

MARTIN. Oh no, not boring at all. I find it, find it all… *fascinating.* I um, I'm a bit of a Scott nerd myself you see. Captain Scott and his gang. Always been fascinated by the stories of Antarctica. You know, the adventure of it all. Wanted to be an explorer myself actually, but

Well….

Ended up in Financial Risk Management, so

He laughs.

I suppose that's what most people say, isn't it? a school project on Scott of the Antarctic and we're all sold.

ALICE. Something like that.

MARTIN. I've always thought it must be an amazing feeling to be down there. Actually boots on the ground, connecting with all that, all that energy around you. It must be incredible.

ALICE. Er, yeah, well it's pretty amazing seeing it in real life. After so long looking at pictures in books.

MARTIN. But being right at the Pole. The energy from the magnetic fields. That must be

ALICE. Er, yeah I guess it's

MARTIN. And the Glossopteris fossils! The ones Scott found. He drags sixteen kilos of them to his death. Sixteen kilos proving the existence of a supercontinent. Those little fossils showing there were once trees on Antarctica.

Incredible.

,

Have you ever

I mean have you ever seen one?

ALICE. Yea, I mean people find different fossils there all the time.

MARTIN. Brilliant. Brilliant. I'd like to, when I go, I'd like to

ALICE (*surprised*). You're going?

MARTIN. Oh well, um. One day. Hopefully.

ALICE. Right…

She looks at him suspiciously.

He reddens.

MARTIN. Because with all these new ice fractures you're finding… Surely they'll expose all kinds of things buried beneath? Who knows what else might be released.

ALICE. Well

MARTIN. Because they think now, don't they, that those fossils, those Glossopteris fossils actually have incredible healing properties. Something about the purity of them I suppose, having been left untouched for so long.

ALICE. Sorry?

MARTIN. Much more powerful than most crystals, they say. Isn't that right?

EVE *appears in the doorway.*

They both look around.

She registers the tension.

EVE. Everything okay?

MARTIN. Yes. I was just finding out about Alice's, about her work.

ALICE. Yes. And I've just been finding out about Martin's fossil theories.

EVE. Ah.

ALICE. Mum. You can't be serious.

EVE. Alice.

ALICE. Don't get me wrong, I'm pleased you're moving on with your life. Meeting new people. But

She gestures to MARTIN.

really?

EVE. You're being very rude. And I was coming down to make things right again.

ALICE. The man thinks fossils have healing powers.

MARTIN. Well

ALICE. Fossils! Which are famously dead.

MARTIN. Well yes but

EVE. I can see no harm in it. If Martin believes that, who are you to tell him that he's wrong?

ALICE. Because he is wrong.

EVE. You wouldn't say that about any other faith. Tell them that what they believe isn't true.

ALICE. That's not

Crystals and energy and good vibes from the Universe aren't a faith.

EVE. To you.

ALICE. To anyone.

And that isn't how energy works. Shoving a fossil up your arse, / or whatever you're suggesting,

MARTIN. / Well, not really how it

EVE. / Alice!

ALICE. isn't a means of generating energy.

EVE. I'm sorry, Martin. She's not usually this horrible.

(*To* ALICE.) It might do you good, you know. To have a bit more faith. Rather than being so pessimistic all the time.

ALICE. You're right. The climate catastrophe is a symptom of people being a bit too morose. Maybe if we all just cheered up, the weather would too.

EVE. Precisely.

ALICE *takes a deep breath.*

ALICE. I just, I don't want you getting caught up in this

In stuff that's just a distraction from

From what's actually going on.

EVE. Here we go.

ALICE. Your house flooded, Mum.

EVE. I know.

ALICE. It's all connected. What's happening in Antarctica

EVE. Don't, Alice. I don't want to hear it. I can't bear it. All this… misery. All the time. You're all the same, you scientists. Just a load of moralistic, high horsing doom-mongerers. The lot of you.

Pause.

ALICE. We got the funding.

EVE. What? Who did?

ALICE. Us. Today. The high horsing doom-mongerers. After our meeting with the NERC. We were in the pub and they called us and they said they'd give it to us. To go back. To keep a team there over winter.

EVE. Today? But

ALICE. Only five of us. But that's all we need really. To monitor it. To work out what it means if this huge chunk collapses. The station will be fine. For now. But it's scary, whatever happens.

EVE. Today? But you only flew back today.

ALICE. I came back a few days ago. I was staying in London.

EVE. You what?

ALICE. I had this meeting today. Emergency funding meeting. They flew me back for it. I had to report on what we'd seen. My analysis of it all.

EVE. You've been back a few days?

ALICE. Yes Mum, but

EVE. A few days and you didn't tell me. Tell Alba.

Electricity.

ALICE. That's not

I have to go back, Mum. Straight away. They need me. It's my

Duty.

And I need you to

I'm asking you to

To

EVE. No.

No. I won't do it.

ALICE. You don't know what I'm

EVE. Of course I do Alice, and the answer is no.

ALICE. But

EVE. You want me to carry on looking after Alba. Well, no. I won't do it.

ALICE. That's

EVE. She's your child.

ALICE. I know.

EVE. Not mine. Not my responsibility.

ALICE. I *know*. I'm not

EVE. I've had forty years of children. Forty years of looking after other people, Alice. And I'm not, I'm actually not going to do it any more.

ALICE. Mum.

EVE. Sorry.

ALICE. I'm not asking for long. A few more months. Over the winter. No more than six

EVE. It's not about that, Alice. It's not about that at all.

ALICE. Then what is it about?

EVE. Your daughter! Abandoning your daughter

ALICE. *Abandoning*?

EVE. Your five-year-old daughter who can't begin to understand why her mother doesn't want to be here to watch her grow up.

ALICE. That's not, that's hardly fair.

People in other countries do this all the time. It's not uncommon for children to be raised by their grandparents in other / parts

EVE. But we're not *in* other parts of the world, Alice. You're not living in some village in central / Africa

ALICE. That's not

EVE. with no electricity, having to walk miles to the nearest water point.

ALICE. I'm not

EVE. They do it because they have no choice. No money, no healthcare if they don't.

ALICE. But we don't have a choice. That's what I'm saying. We're at a point now where that choice is gone.

'

Please, Mum you

You owe me this.

EVE. ,

Owe you?

ALICE. Your generation. You owe us a future. A chance at one at least.

EVE *laughs.*

EVE. You're joking.

ALICE. And I owe Alba. I'm asking for your help. I need your help, Mum.

EVE. I don't owe you anything. You have no idea what I've done for you.

For this family.

I owe you nothing, Alice. It's my turn for life now. Understand? My turn.

Silence.

EVE *and* ALICE *look daggers at each other.*

MARTIN *rocks nervously side to side.*

MARTIN. Perhaps we should all just

The women round on MARTIN.

EVE *and* ALICE. Yes?

MARTIN. ,

Nothing.

EVE. ,

Martin and I are going away.

ALICE. What? When?

EVE. In a few weeks. We're going on a cruise.

MARTIN. Oh. I thought we weren't going to

ALICE. *A cruise?*

EVE. To Antarctica. South America.

ALICE. *A cruise?*

EVE. Yes, Alice.

ALICE. To Antarctica?

EVE. And South America. We're very excited about it. Aren't we, Martin?

MARTIN. Er yes. Though perhaps this isn't the / best

ALICE. You won't help me with Alba because you're going on holiday?

EVE. No. I won't help you with Alba *and* I'm going on holiday.

ALICE. Look, I understand you need your own life, your own

But this is my *work*. Can't you just, can't you at least postpone it?

EVE. No. We can't. We don't want to.

ALICE. Well then!

She throws up her hands in mock surrender.

EVE. I thought you

I thought you might actually be pleased.

ALICE. Pleased? Why would I be

EVE. Because. I'm taking an interest in your work. That's what you've wanted for years, isn't it? Well now I am. I want to see where you've been going. See what you've seen, what you've been telling me about so passionately all this time. I thought that's what you wanted.

ALICE. Why would I

I don't want that. This isn't you taking an interest in my work, this is you actively making my work harder. Do you, can you even *comprehend* the damage those things do? The effect they're having on our

EVE. Of course, I'm not stupid but

ALICE. You know what. I actually think you are. Stupid. I think you're not actually very bright at all and you're punishing me for being clever.

EVE. Oh really?

ALICE. For doing a job you could never have done. For actually going away and pursuing something I love, that I'm good at. Because you never got to.

A cruise?

ALICE *reels for a moment.*

Then she snaps.

Fine.

She goes to the freezer and pulls out a tub of ice cream.

EVE. What are you doing? What are you doing with that?

ALICE. It's obviously not sinking in so why don't I just show you?

She up ends the ice cream on the kitchen table.

EVE. Oh god, Alice!

ALICE *scoops out a section of the bottom edge of the ice cream block.*

She leaves a shelf jutting out from the main block.

ALICE. So here. Here's the ice sheet, right? Which sits on the bedrock.

EVE*'s eyes water slightly.*

ALICE *indicates the newly created shelf.*

And this stuff here, which floats on the ocean water, is ice *shelf.* If that breaks off…

She pulls a quantity of ice cream off the end of the 'shelf'.

Dumps the handful down on the table.

EVE *groans.*

that becomes an iceberg, right? And in theory that's okay, because this is already ice that's floating. It's not contributing any more weight into the sea at this point.

But the problem is, it's a cork out of a bottle effect. You start removing this part (the ice shelf), and the ice behind it becomes more vulnerable.

And the bit we've been looking at is down here. The Grounding Line, where the ice sheet sits on the bedrock (the table in this case). Because the oceans are getting so much warmer, the water is starting to melt the ice, which means the grounding line is retreating…

She hacks at the bottom of the 'Glacier' where the ice cream meets the table.

And now we've got surface meltwater too. Which is the other thing that's started to happen.

She pours some of the whiskey onto the top of the ice cream.

She forms a small 'lake'.

Melt ponds which used to just occur in Greenland are now appearing in Antarctica – these big lakes and rivers forming on the ice sheet. The water gets into cracks in the ice and forces the ice shelves apart. *Hydrofracture.* There's greater pressure in water than ice, so the weight of the water in the cracks drives them open like forcing a wedge down them. Like…

She puts a spoon into the heart of the ice cream block and hits her palm down on top of it.

It breaks apart.

So the combination of these two processes means we're losing ice into the oceans at a potentially uncontrollable rate. And soon…

Ta da!

She gestures to the annihilated block of ice cream on the table.

EVE *looks at her in horror.* MARTIN *with some fascination.*

Silence.

EVE. HAVE YOU GONE COMPLETELY MAD?

Pause.

ALICE. Maybe.

Maybe I have.

It feels like fucking madness half the time. Being down there. Seeing what we're seeing and then coming back here. Back home where nobody seems to care. Where, however much we shout about it, however much we bang our fucking heads against the walls, no one wants to listen.

So yeah.

Maybe that is the definition of madness.

*

But it's a madness I need to be part of.

The sound of crying from off stage.

Both ALICE *and* EVE *turn towards the sound of the noise.*

Then ALICE *looks to* EVE, *terrified.*

Mum.

*

I can't.

EVE. What?

ALICE. I can't, I can't.

EVE. Don't be so silly, of course you

ALICE. I can't go up there. Please, Mum.

EVE. What are you talking about? She's your daughter.

ALICE. Yes.

EVE. Your daughter who you haven't seen once. Not once since you got back. Not once gone upstairs to see her.

ALICE. I can't. I can't.

EVE. Why not? Why not, Alice?

ALICE. Because I know. I know, I know, I know that if I go upstairs and see her, I'll break in two. If she wraps her little fingers around mine and calls my name I'll never be able to go back again.

And I need to go back, Mum. I have to.

I have to, I have to, I

EVE *stares at her.*

EVE. You need to sort yourself out, Alice.

Whatever this

Whatever's going on.

You need to sort it out. Because this

This is

ALICE *looks at her, pleadingly.*

Fine.

EVE *goes to the door leading upstairs, then stops. Turns back.*

You know you make it out like you're some kind of martyr going down there. Some kind of superhero, saving the planet. But you're no different than the rest of us. You go because you want to. Because you enjoy it. Because it excites you. And that's fair enough, Alice.

But you could at least be honest about it.

She exits.

ALICE *stands rigid. Looking at the door leading upstairs.*

MARTIN *watches her awkwardly.*

MARTIN. Alice

ALICE. I'm really good at my job.

MARTIN. I I know.

ALICE. I'm the leading expert in what I do. I'm the only one, actually, who can do this specific job. And I've worked really fucking hard to get here.

MARTIN. I know that.

She puts a hand on the door leading upstairs.

ALICE. But I would give all of that up instantly if she asked me to.

If Alba

If she

,

I haven't been able to think about her To let myself think about her while I

I've just had to put her in a box and forget about her because otherwise I think my heart would have

Out of my chest.

Pause.

MARTIN. I understand.

ALICE. No you

I'm sorry but you

You really don't.

She goes to sit at the kitchen table.

She pours herself another large whiskey and gulps it down.

MARTIN *hovers.*

MARTIN. I left my kids. Once.

Walked away.

ALICE. ,

When?

MARTIN. When they were four and two.

ALICE. Why?

MARTIN (*shrugs*). I got scared.

ALICE. Oh.

MARTIN. Yeah.

ALICE. That's not the same.

MARTIN. No.

ALICE. What you did was awful.

MARTIN. Yes.

ALICE. What I'm doing is

,

It's not the same.

MARTIN. No. I know.

Pause.

ALICE. What happened?

MARTIN. I came back.

I left for four days. Got on a train up to Newcastle. Stayed in a Premiere Inn. Day one, I thought – *this is freedom.* Day two, I thought about killing myself. Day three, I tried to kill myself. Day four, I got back on the train and came home.

Pause.

ALICE. Wow.

MARTIN. Yeah.

ALICE. What about your wife? Did she

MARTIN. Oh, yeah. She never forgave me. Why would she? It was unforgivable. But it cured me of all my fear. Of being a father, of being trapped, of of

I just needed to get it out of my system, I guess. At her expense. At their expense too, I suppose.

Pause.

ALICE. That's not

You know that's not what I'm doing, right?

MARTIN. I know.

ALICE. ,

Maybe she's right. Mum. Maybe that is what I want. To be a hero. For Alba to look back one day and think that I did something incredible. Something no one else could.

,

And maybe that's mad.

But isn't that what everyone wants? For scientists to be the heroes? To find the answer. Invent something. Discover something. Flick a switch and solve it all.

Christ, *I* want that.

But all I turned out to be was a prophet. A moralistic, high horsing, doom-mongering climate scientist.

Nothing more.

ALICE *looks at the albatross.*

She moves warily towards it.

Is it an omen?

Is that why you brought it?

MARTIN. No! No, they're good luck symbols. Aren't they? Traditionally. And I thought

Perhaps wrongly, but I thought

I thought it might be something you'd like. A reminder. Of your time there.

,

I know you think it's all

That I'm a bit

But finding my place in the Universe. Finding my spirituality. My connection to the Earth, to nature, to to

Well it's helped me find a connection to other people too. And that's that's pulled me out of a dark place more than once and so I thought

I thought maybe

I thought maybe this might

Having a connection to *there* while you're *here*, might make you feel

Might give you that kind of connection too.

They look at each other. A moment of shared recognition.

Then ALICE *goes to him and kisses him.*

He is paralysed for a moment, then suddenly breaks away.

He pushes her back.

Oh god. Oh no.

Alice, I

ALICE. I'm sorry. Sorry, I

MARTIN. No, I

My fault I was

,

I love Eve. Very much. I know it hasn't been

Well not very long in the grand scheme of things but I do think the absolute, the absolute world of her.

ALICE. I know.

MARTIN. And she, she deserves to be happy. To be looked after for once. And I'd like to be that for her. I think I could be that for her.

ALICE. I'm sure you are. I'm sorry.

MARTIN. Alice.

He touches her shoulder, kindly. Conciliatory.

She moves away, embarrassed.

Goes to the sink and gets a cloth.

ALICE. I should

I need to clear this up

I

She starts trying to clear up the ice cream on the table.

If anything she's making it worse. Smearing it all over the place.

MARTIN. Alice.

ALICE. God, what a mess. What a

EVE *appears in the doorway.*

She looks at ALICE *and* MARTIN. *They look at her.*

Silence.

EVE. All all right?

ALICE. Yeah. Yeah, fine.

Is she

Can't she sleep?

EVE. No she's just

I said I'd bring her up some milk.

ALICE. I'll do it.

EVE. Really?

ALICE. Yeah. I'll take it up to her.

EVE. ,

Okay.

Pause.

ALICE. Warm milk or

EVE. Just from the fridge is fine. She doesn't need much. Don't give her too much or she'll

,

You've got it.

ALICE *goes to the fridge and takes out the milk.*

She gets a glass and pours a small amount into the bottom of it.

She takes the milk and leaves, heading upstairs.

A short silence.

Was she being rude to you again?

MARTIN. Oh no, no. Nothing like that.

EVE. Just ignore her. She gets like this when she's upset. When she's angry. Just the same as her father.

Maybe I supported her too much? Encouraged her to follow her dreams. Do whatever she wanted. Maybe that was overwhelming.

My mother never did.

Never had that growing up. Just had to get on with it myself. And that was hard. So I tried to be better with her. Show her more love than my mother ever showed me. But maybe that backfired.

,

I was on track to be a dancer, Martin. Did I tell you that?

MARTIN. You did, yes.

EVE. I did. Well I was. Only chorus line mostly. But it was mine. My thing. Which I was good at. Which I loved.

But then I met her dad and well

,

She'll never understand what I gave up to be her mother.

EVE *starts to clear up loudly.*

Each movement is deliberate and rather forceful.

MARTIN *stands awkwardly, watching her.*

She scrapes the remainder of Alice's rice pudding into the bin.

She runs the tap and squeezes washing up liquid into each bowl to soak.

MARTIN. I'm sure she

Even if she doesn't quite

Doesn't understand the full extent

EVE. She doesn't.

MARTIN. Even so, I'm sure she's very grateful

EVE. She's not.

MARTIN. Oh.

EVE. I'm sorry, Martin. But she can't begin to understand the sacrifices I've made.

MARTIN *nods slowly.*

MARTIN. And you don't think she's making a sacrifice of her own?

EVE *stops for a moment.*

Then resumes her tidying.

She attacks the rice pudding pan with a scourer.

EVE. Forgot to soak this. It's already like cement.

MARTIN. Let me

EVE. It's fine.

Martin.

It's fine.

MARTIN. Okay.

EVE. If she wasn't so bloody stubborn and difficult, maybe that good-for-nothing husband of hers wouldn't have run so far away. Maybe *he* would be looking after their daughter now. Not me.

ALICE *appears in the doorway.*

MARTIN *looks mortified.*

ALICE. Her hair is so long.

,

You were right, Mum. I can't

This is

Here. This is where I'm meant to be.

I shouldn't have left her with you. I'm sorry.

I'm going to call them. Say I can't

I'm not going back. They'll have to find someone else.

EVE. Oh.

,

Oh right.

ALICE *hesitates, phone in hand.*

Then she exits.

MARTIN *looks at* EVE. *She avoids his eye.*

What a mess. She always leaves such a mess.

She starts mopping the table.

MARTIN. Eve…

EVE. Hasn't changed. Not since she was a child. Always breaking things and spilling things. Alba's the same. They're just the same those two, really.

MARTIN. Eve…

EVE. Peas in a

She stops what she's doing. Looks at him.

Puts down the cloth.

Where will we go first?

MARTIN. When?

She walks to him.

Puts her arms around him.

EVE. When we cruise? Where's first?

MARTIN. Oh. Argentina.

EVE. Mm.

MARTIN. Then the Falklands.

EVE. Yes.

MARTIN. South Georgia, along the Scotia Sea.

EVE. Yes.

MARTIN. Then down to the Antarctic peninsular.

EVE. And what will we see?

MARTIN. Oh dolphins and humpback whales, seals and penguins. Even an albatross or two maybe.

EVE *laughs.*

EVE. And where will we sleep?

MARTIN. Up on the top deck. Every night.

EVE. Every night?

MARTIN. Yeah. Camped out on sunloungers in eternal
daylight.

EVE. Mm. That's nice.

MARTIN. Yeah.

EVE kisses him.

Then breaks away.

EVE. I was rude to her. Earlier. It was unfair of me.

Her love isn't warm like mine. It's a battle cry. An
unstoppable force.

She goes to the albatross.

She looks at it warily – a mix of fear and reverence.

They told us we could have it all.

They lied.

Pause.

MARTIN. We're not going, are we?

EVE. I'm sorry, Martin.

MARTIN. It's okay.

EVE. It's not.

MARTIN. No, really it's

EVE. It was lovely to dream. With you. To be someone else
for a while. To be a version of me that I've always, that I
thought I could be but I

MARTIN. I understand.

She smiles at him.

EVE. You should still go. On the cruise.

MARTIN. Oh.

Um, well

EVE. Oh yes, sorry. Of course you were going to go.

MARTIN. No I

I mean I

EVE. Perhaps you'll find one of your fossils?

MARTIN. Perhaps, yeah.

,

Eve. I really did

EVE. I know.

,

Me too.

He nods. Exits.

EVE *watches after him for a moment, then sits down at the table.*

She unscrews the whiskey bottle and drinks straight from it.

She grimaces.

ALICE *enters. She watches her mum from the doorway.*

EVE *senses her behind her.*

All all right with your colleagues, was it?

ALICE. Er, yeah. Yeah, fine. They understand.

EVE. Right.

ALICE. I just passed Martin. Is that

Did something happen?

,

Mum?

EVE. Whiskey?

ALICE. ,

Sure.

EVE *pours a glass for* ALICE.

ALICE *gets another glass for* EVE.

They both sit at the table and drink.

EVE. Awful stuff, this.

ALICE. I know.

EVE. Now we know why he drank it with Dr Pepper.

ALICE *laughs.*

They both take another drink.

They look at the albatross.

It looks back at them.

Funny things, aren't they? Albatrosses.

ALICE. Yeah.

EVE. Just big seagulls really.

ALICE. Basically.

Where did he get it from?

EVE. Auction house down in London somewhere. Said he just stumbled across it, but I reckon he was looking for one for months. Supposedly for me. Supposedly my gift but I

I think he's been obsessed with the idea of you since the moment we met.

ALICE. Oh.

EVE. ,

Cost him a fortune too.

ALICE. Did it?

EVE. An absolute fortune.

Pause.

Then EVE *starts laughing.*

ALICE. What?

EVE. I don't know.

ALICE. What's so funny?

EVE. I don't know I just

She's really laughing now, doubled up.

ALICE. Mum?

ALICE is laughing now too. The laughter is infectious.

EVE. Sorry, it's just

It's just he doesn't drive, Martin.

ALICE. So?

EVE. So he must have had it on the tube.

Must have had that *thing* sat next to him on the tube. Oh the Circle Line. Then on the train up here.

She's wheezing. She can't breathe.

Martin, and his stuffed albatross.

ALICE is laughing hard now too.

Tears roll down their cheeks.

Then suddenly they're not anymore.

The laughter subsides.

They sit in silence for a moment.

ALICE. Mum, I'm

EVE. It's all right.

ALICE. It's not. I'm sorry. Really. I just

,

I don't know how to do both. To *be* both.

EVE. But you are. You already are.

EVE takes ALICE*'s hands. She holds them tightly in her own.*

They look at each other for a moment. An understanding.

Go on now. While it's still night. While it's all still a dream.

A moment, then she breaks, practical again.

ALICE *looks at her, stunned.*

ALICE. But

What about

What about the cruise?

EVE. There'll be others.

She smiles.

Besides. I've got some Peter Rabbit ears to finish.

,

They've been a real bastard to make.

EVE *goes to a cupboard and pulls out a sewing box and a half-made set of bunny ears.*

She sits in the armchair and begins sewing.

ALICE *hesitates, watching* EVE.

She goes to the albatross. Lays a hand on the top of it.

Then she goes to the hallway, picking up her rucksack.

She takes a final look around the kitchen. At EVE. *Then goes.*

The sound of the front door opening.

A huge gust of snow tears through into the kitchen, surrounding EVE.

The albatross is illuminated on its table.

Then the front door closes offstage.

A Nick Hern Book

Albatross first published in Great Britain as a paperback original in 2026
by Nick Hern Books Limited, The Glasshouse, 49a Goldhawk Road, London
W12 8QP, in association with Menagerie Theatre

Albatross copyright © 2026 Martha Loader

Martha Loader has asserted her right to be identified as the author of this work

Cover photograph: Alejandro Gaytan via Shutterstock

Designed and typeset by Nick Hern Books, London
Printed in Great Britain by Mimeo Ltd, Huntingdon, Cambridgeshire PE29 6XX

A CIP catalogue record for this book is available from the British Library

ISBN 978 1 83904 559 2

www.nickhernbooks.co.uk/environmental-policy

Nick Hern Books' authorised representative in the EU is
Easy Access System Europe – Mustamäe tee 50, 10621 Tallinn, Estonia
email gpsr.requests@easproject.com